Library of Congress Catalog Card
Number 96-75930
ISBN 1-56647-118-4
Design by Jane Hopkins
First Printing, October 1996
1 2 3 4 5 6 7 8 9

Mutual Publishing
1127 11th Avenue, Mezz. B
Honolulu, Hawaii 96816
Ph: (808) 732-1709
Fax: (808) 734-4094
Email: mutual@lava.net
URL: http://www.pete.com/mutual

Printed in Taiwan

HAWAI'I'S
NATURAL
Wonders

TEXT BY JAN TENBRUGGENCATE
PHOTOGRAPHY BY DOUGLAS PEEBLES

Plunging cliffs and plummeting waterfalls along the Big Island of Hawai'i's North Kohala coastline display a cause and effect of the erosion that has shaped much of the Hawaiian landscape.

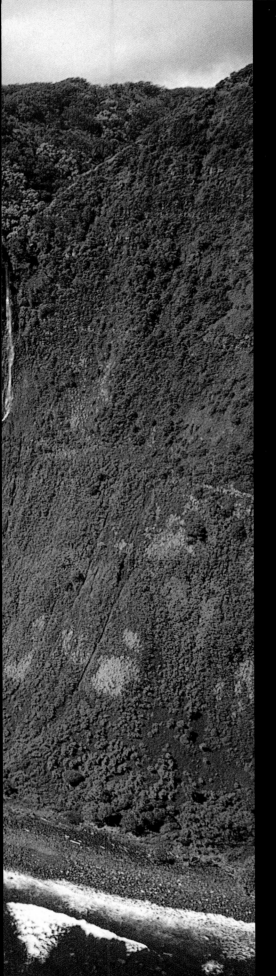

TABLE *of* CONTENTS

Moloka'i's northern coast, placid in summer and raging with storm surf in winter, provides a lesson in the effects of erosion on Hawaiian volcanic islands.

INTRODUCTION

If you were to build a paradise, you'd start with isolation.

It would be a place where the rest of the world could intrude only with great difficulty.

Pick the biggest ocean in the world and find a spot in the middle of it, where it's warm, but where trade winds blow cooling breezes almost the year around.

There you find Hawai'i, the world's most isolated chain of islands.

It's 2,400 miles from the nearest continental landfall to the east and 3,800 miles to the west. Far to the north are the chilly Aleutians and Alaska and, to the south, the first continent you'll reach is Antarctica.

Build this paradise solid, using rock from deep in the earth's mantle, thrown up in spectacular, fiery displays. Build a chain of islands, each sufficiently different so no one island encompasses all the wonders.

Provide long, deep beaches, and small, private coves. Wide bays fringed with palms, and rocky inlets shaded by steep cliffs where seabirds nest.

Give it North Pacific swells crashing in snowy displays onto black seacliffs. Calm waters protected by coastal reefs, where flashy fishes cluster around coral heads.

Inland, provide mysterious dark rivers, creeping through overhanging vegetation. And dry, rock-strewn streambeds that only occasionally roar with flash floods.

And waterfalls, and ferny cliffs dripping with brilliant droplets from natural springs.

Cloak this paradise with both rain forests and deserts, with plants not found anywhere else in the world, and multicolored birds. From the raspberries, take away the thorns. From plants with toxic parentage, take away the poisons.

Give this place a few high mountains where the snow sometimes falls, but give most of it a t-shirt-and-shorts kind of climate.

Give it sunrises over the eastern sea, and sunsets that drop into the sea to the west.

Find this spot, build it in your mind.

Open your eyes.

There, you find Hawai'i.

In this volume, you'll find photographs and descriptions of these Islands—this paradise.

And just as our own views of paradise evolve with time, you'll find that the real Hawai'i evolves. It's a work in progress.

Parts of Hawai'i are millions of years old.

And parts are just minutes old, smoking and cracking as the fresh lava cools.

The flow of molten rock into the sea during the eruption at Kilauea's East Rift Zone creates clouds of acid steam. The lava is instantly solidified upon hitting the water. Some of it shatters into tiny crystals, which wash back ashore to create glistening black sand beaches.

Sea waves create a crust when they wash up onto the molten lava, but the pressure of the flow cracks it open, and the red-orange rock oozes out in fiery lava falls.

VOLCANOES

The little twin-engine plane banked close alongside the lava fountain on the rift of Kilauea, Hawai'i's most active volcano. Cameras clicked. It was night, and the sight of this bright orange pillar was surreal.

It looked like a giant water fountain bathed in orange light. But even inside the plane, pilot and passengers could feel the heat. Later they would find that the paint had blistered on the underside of the plane's wings.

Trees were aflame as the lava pooled and poured through the 'ohi'a forest. The trunks of some live trees, their moisture superheated, exploded in loud blasts.

THE DEVELOPMENT OF THE HAWAIIAN CHAIN

The Hawaiian chain has been under construction for some 70 million years, although the two oldest of the main islands, Kaua'i and Ni'ihau, are in the neighborhood of just five million years old.

Older islands, extending 1,400 miles to the northwest, have eroded down to small rocks and atolls. And still older ones have slipped beneath the sea. These latter islands, including the Emperor Seamounts, stretch all the way to the Aleutian trench.

Overall, from the Big Island of Hawai'i to the Meiji Seamount, the Hawaiian chain extends some 3,600 miles.

To understand the development of the island chain, visualize a sheet of paper held over a candle. The paper represents the Pacific plate, one of a series of slowly moving plates that form the surface of the planet.

The plate is moving slowly, driven by the stresses of neighboring plates and volcanic activity at its rim. Beneath the plate is a hot spot, represented by the candle.

Start with the candle under one corner of the page and move the paper diagonally. As the paper is moved in one direction over the candle's flame, it occasionally burns through, creating a line of blackened holes in the paper.

Similarly, a hot spot deep in the earth creates stresses in the ocean floor, which cracks open. Magma, the geologist's term for underground molten rock, breaks through, and the process of island-building begins. As the Pacific plate moves on, the formation of that island ceases and, at a new opening, another island begins.

If you change the direction in which the paper is moving, the line of black spots moves as well. In the Hawaiian archipelago, the plate was moving northward from about 70 million years ago to about 43 million years ago. Then, the forces around the Pacific changed, and the plate began moving northwesterly. As a result, if you were to sail along the route of the archipelago's creation, you'd head northwest from Hawai'i, past the main islands, beyond French Frigate Shoals and Midway, and finally past Kure Atoll, the last speck of dry Hawaiian land. You'd sail another 500 miles, then you'd turn north. And if you

A lava fountain at the Pu'u 'o'o vent on Kilauea's East Rift Zone feeds a river of red flowing molten rock.

had a powerful depth-recording device, you could pick up the rise and fall of the ocean floor as you passed over the seamounts that represent Hawai'i's ancient history.

ERUPTIONS

When the Hawaiian Islands begin forming, you never know it from evidence on the surface. The eruptions remain thousands of feet below sea level and the fluid lavas pile up, one atop the next, forming a huge underwater volcano. The next Hawaiian island, Loihi, is now being formed in this way. It's in just over 3,000 feet of water, about 22 miles off the Big Island's Ka'u coastline. Researchers check in constantly, keeping sensitive equipment permanently installed in the deep ocean to track the activity of this infant island. Additionally, there are occasional visits by submersible craft.

Over the centuries, the height of seamounts like Loihi rises with the regular eruptions. When the volcano nears the sea surface, dramatic explosions create huge volumes of ash, which settle around the center of the eruption. Islands that stop their development at this phase erode easily. They are made primarily of hardened ash, known as tuff. They often form crescent islets, like Molokini off Maui and Lehua off Ni'ihau, in which one section of the formerly circular cone has been eaten away.

On those islands that get beyond this state, most of the eruption is now occurring above water, and the eruptions lose much of their violence. One lava flow after another coats the land, giving it a hard, black rock shell, and the young island with steep underwater flanks is transformed by its continued eruptions into a huge, shallow-sided shield volcano. Mauna Loa and Kilauea are in this phase. While the summit is normally the center of major activity, much of the surface activity can occur on rift zones, great arms that extend out from the volcano summits.

THE CYCLE OF CREATION AND DESTRUCTION

Creation is a violent process, and the violence affects new arrivals to the islands. By this stage in an island's development, it will be filled with life. Seeds and spores have arrived on the wind and sea. Birds and bugs have flown or been blown in. The islands for millions of years have been coated in vegetation, but by the time the volcanic chain started to appear, it was not necessary for each new island to be populated from the distant continents. Once a species arrived on one island, moving to another nearby island was much easier, but researchers have not found that many Hawaiian species leapfrogged from one island to the next.

An eruption destroys some of this life. New eruptions cover nearby vegetation with ash and rock. Lava flows snake through forests, burning all in their wake. If lava reaches the sea, the molten rock flows out over the reefs, sets the sea aboil, and creates black-sand beaches that cover the habitat of coast-dwelling species.

In recent times, eruptions have been disruptive to human life as well.

The long-running eruption on Kilauea's East Rift Zone that started in 1982 not only draped hundreds of acres of formerly forested land in a shroud of smooth *pahoehoe* and broken *'a'a* lava, but it destroyed a community.

Kalapana was a traditional Hawaiian fishing village that in the 1970's also became home to a cluster of back-to-the-earth folks and a smattering of Mainland retirees. The nearby hillside subdivision of Royal Gardens had no utilities and was largely undeveloped, but a few folks lived there, catching rainwater and producing their light from lanterns or generators.

The eruption that created the cone at Pu'u 'o'o changed that. It sent flow after flow down the side of Kilauea toward the sea. Residents sat in the night and watched the orange glow as the flows hissed and smoked down the mountainside.

One home after another burst into flames as the molten rock crept around their foundation posts. Efforts to stop the lava by spraying water on the advancing flow were fruitless. By the end of a decade, the whole of Kalapana was gone. The popular natural pool called Queen's Bath was filled with black rock. The visitor center at the Waha'ula *heiau* was burned, although, remarkably, the lava stayed out of the *heiau* itself.

Parishioners managed to prop up the historic Kalapana Painted Church, get beams under it, and move it out of the way of the advancing flow. Residents piled their belongings on trucks and hauled them away.

The eruption was unrelenting. Year after year, it piled on the lava. It flowed into the sea, where clouds of acid steam billowed forth. It built acres and acres of new land. This, volcano scientists now say, may have been the norm during the Islands' shield-building phase.

The lava flow travels miles down the mountainside, sometimes on the surface and sometimes in enclosed lava tubes, to finally reach the sea.

EROSION AND SUBSIDENCE

Eventually, on a scale of tens and hundreds of thousands of years, the volcanic activity slows. The millennia pass, and the new island, firmly attached to the ocean floor, is dragged away from the Hawaiian hot spot as the Pacific plate moves northwestward. While there are still occasional eruptions, they are infrequent, and the island begins eroding. Hualalai on Hawai'i and Haleakala on Maui have erupted within human memory, but it's been two centuries.

The tops of some volcanoes collapse, forming great calderas. The most famous of these is the Haleakala caldera, which is a favorite spot over which to view the sunrise. If you drive to the rim of Haleakala, now the site of a national park, you can look out into the caldera and see a topography that looks like nothing so much as the surface of the moon. Few writers can resist the temptation to call it "lunar." The crater contains more than 12,500 acres and is more than 3,000 feet deep, from its lowest point to the highest point of the rim of the crater.

Haleakala is a typical shield volcano. From the summit vantage, its huge bulk slopes gradually from the edges of the caldera down to the sea—a great, shallow dome.

If you turn the other way and look out across the isthmus to West Maui, the scene is very different. This older volcano has been eaten away by time, wind and water. It has deeply cut valleys and narrow, jagged peaks. The windward side of Haleakala, much more subject to erosion than the western slope, has a similar look.

At this point, erosion and subsidence become major factors in the geological history of the islands.

The immense weight of the islands causes the ocean floor to sag, creating a deep area around the larger islands. This sag means the newer islands themselves are sinking with respect to the sea surface. To residents, it appears that the ocean is gradually rising. (Actually, this is happening, too, and the combination of the sinking of the islands and the rising of the seas creates shoreline erosion problems that will be discussed later in this volume).

Rain, wind and waves eat away at the islands. Deep valleys appear, landslides dump broken rock and mud into valley floors, and storms flush it all out into the sea. At the shore, waves cut away at the edges of the island, forming seacliffs. Great earth movements sometimes crack off large sections of islands and send them crashing into the sea. Sophisticated underwater mapping techniques show evidence of incredible landslides that extend tens of miles out into the sea, the rocky debris spread out like great fans on the ocean floor.

But the volcanic activity isn't entirely over.

THE SECONDARY PERIOD OF VOLCANIC ACTIVITY

Long after an island is severely eroded and appears volcanically dead, there is often a secondary period of volcanic activity. Fresh lava bursts through cracks in flows hundreds of thousands of years old and the resulting fountaining builds up circular piles of ash and cinder. The evidence is in the form of volcanic cones that dot the islands. Famed Diamond Head and Punchbowl on O'ahu, known to Hawaiians as Le'ahi and Puowaina, are such features. Similar cones are visible on all the larger islands. Even the oldest of the major islands, Kaua'i, has plenty of evidence of this late volcanic activity in Kilohana Crater, lying between Nawiliwili and Wai'ale'ale, and Crater Hill at Kilauea.

Eventually the island is far enough from the hot spot that no new volcanic activity is possible. Now it is in a state of permanent erosive decline. Islands continue to sink and to diminish in size until they are little more than oceanic rocks, like Nihoa and Necker, northwest of Kaua'i.

As they decline further, their coral reefs are all that remain. As long as the corals grow as fast as the island subsides, an atoll remains. Midway and Kure Atolls are examples.

Kure is the last speck of dry land in the Hawaiian archipelago. Beyond it, in the cooler waters where coral doesn't grow well, are the long-lost Hawaiian islands; the seamounts that have dipped below the wash of the waves.

A slow-moving lava flow at Kalapana wraps around doomed coconut palms, and lobes of the flow fill in low areas.

The summit of Hualalai, Hawai'i, peeks above the clouds in the distance. This volcano has not erupted in nearly two centuries, but seismic activity indicates it is still alive.

A helicopter hovers over a skylight, a hole in the ceiling of a lava tube system that provides visual access to the subsurface flow.

The eroding craters at the summit of Hualalai, Hawai'i are clothed in sparse vegetation.

The caldera of Haleakala, Maui, features numerous cinder cones that are evidence of secondary volcanic activity.

A snowy winter day atop Mauna Kea, considered by astronomers to be one of the best sites in the world for observing the heavens. Several observatories are visible at the summit. Mauna Kea rises nearly 14,000 feet above sea level and has an alpine environment. During cooler global climate conditions, the mountain has supported an ice cap on several occasions.

A helicopter flies along the steeply eroded cliff faces and valleys of Kaua'i's Na Pali Coast.

*L*ANDFORMS

One of Hawai'i's most intriguing physical characteristics is the vertical definition of its islands. In the middle of this vast expanse of sea, these islands, unlike many of the atolls of the South Pacific, surge upward, catching clouds and even creating some of their own weather.

Even when the trade winds aren't blowing, which is seldom, the islands create their own wind. At night, the land cools more quickly than the sea, and the denser cool mountain air blows down the valleys, as if the islands were exhaling. In the day, the land warms faster than the sea and the warmed air over the land rises. More air is pulled in from over the water to replace it, creating an onshore breeze. And the islands appear to breathe back in.

The high elevations and the relative small size of the islands give residents the opportunity to change their climate in short order. On average there is a 3-degree Fahrenheit drop in temperature for every 1,000-foot gain in elevation. It means that swimsuit weather is often within an hour's drive of coat weather.

EXPERIENCE HAWAI'I'S VERTICAL DEFINITION

The main islands are all high islands, a term used to separate them from atolls and reefs. But the Hawaiian high islands display their vertical sides in different ways.

∾ Stand along the coast in Hilo and look up nearly 14,000 feet to the summit of Mauna Kea, far above the lowest clouds. See amid the snowy slopes a cluster of little white balls. These are a group of world-class astronomical observatories.

∾ Or, for a contrasting view, stand at the chilly summit of Mauna Kea and look down on the cloud tops, and pick out a distant speck of shoreline.

∾ View from the beach at Pa'ia, Maui, the gentle, long slope of Haleakala, again, up into the clouds.

∾ Walk around the eroded, red-earth summit of Kaho'olawe and feel how the dry island falls away on all sides to a blue sea, not far in any direction.

∾ At Shipwreck Beach on Lana'i, look upward at a rocky, rising terrain. Though it's a small island, as you climb inland and upward, the horizon keeps moving, up and away, until finally you reach the little summit forest.

∾ Panting, after a long climb to the rim of Wailau Valley on Moloka'i, you are left doubly breathless by the sheer steepness and height of its walls.

∾ From the campus of the University of Hawai'i at Manoa, look up into Manoa Valley, see a green-walled cathedral with an overarching blue sky.

∾ When the clouds clear at Kilohana, at the edge of Kaua'i's Alaka'i Swamp, Wainiha Valley falls away and you can check out the surf in Hanalei Bay.

∾ Ni'ihau has vast flatlands near sea level at its northern and southern ends, and its compact mountain mass springs up suddenly in between.

These are all ways of experiencing Hawai'i's vertical definition. Each brings up different emotions, enhances the senses differently.

The jagged mountain ridgeline of the Ha'upu Range on Kaua'i is so narrow in places that a climber can sit with one leg over each side.

THE ISLANDS' CLIFFS

Some of the Islands' most spectacular features are its sea cliffs. And those of the north shore of East Moloka'i are the most impressive of all. The Guiness Book of World Records credits them with being the highest sea cliffs in the world.

Camping at their base means seeing very little sunshine. Even in summer, the rising sun and the setting sun can be hidden behind the Island, and only in the middle of the day is the full sun visible.

In winter, this windward side of the Island is cold, dark and wet.

The cliff faces, cut by dramatic valleys, sweep up from sea level to as high as 3,600 feet. Kahiwa, the longest waterfall in Hawai'i, cascades 1,750 feet down one of these cliffs.

Narrow bands of talus at the base of the north Moloka'i cliffs once housed a substantial Native Hawaiian population. Remnants of their agricultural terraces, temples and house sites remain. The main inhabitants today, though, are the introduced goats that steadily munch away at the Island's rare native plants and whose trails crisscross the cliff faces.

On the Big Island, many of the stages of erosion are visible, from the sea undercutting still-steaming, fresh lava benches at the shoreline, to the deep, green valleys of the Kohala Mountains. Kohala is the oldest of the Big Island's volcanoes at about a quarter of a million years of age.

O'ahu, older than both Moloka'i and Hawai'i, is made up of the remains of two volcanoes, which formed the Ko'olau mountains and the Wai'anae chain. But like the north shore of east Moloka'i, the north side of the eastern Ko'olau mountains is missing, having disappeared into the sea, leaving incredibly steep, tall cliffs. In the ocean for up to 40 miles off both Moloka'i and O'ahu, you can find the rubble of the missing section of the island, strewn across the sea floor as the result of being exposed to millions of years of active fault lines, earth shudders and undercutting by the sea.

Deep in the ocean between the islands, there are still geologic mysteries. During the 1950's, planes flying between Kaua'i and O'ahu reported seeing the sea boiling, and passengers reported smelling sulfur. It had all the indications of a volcanic eruption, but this part of the

Hawaiian chain is more than 200 miles from the Hawaiian hot spot, and two miles deep. The event was forgotten until the mid-1990's, when a survey crew photographing the ocean floor reported finding a fresh-looking lava flow on the sea floor of the Ka'ie'ie Waho Channel, better known today as the Kaua'i Channel.

THE EFFECTS OF THE TRADE WINDS

The high islands stand in the path of the trade winds, the name for that nearly constant flow of breezes that carried early sailing ships south along the North American coastline and then westward across the Pacific. The winds are still used by sailors taking the easy downwind run to Hawai'i.

As the trades, rich with moisture picked up from the sea, reach the islands, they are driven up the slopes. With the increasing altitude, the air cools and, since the cooled air can no longer support the high humidity, clouds form and the rain falls on the windward sides of the higher islands. These rains have driven the erosive forces that over the eons have eaten away at the windward sides. They are the reasons that the northwest sides of Hawai'i, Maui, Moloka'i, O'ahu and Kaua'i are so green and so dramatically cut with deep valleys slung between precipitous cliffs.

So what of the other islands—Kaho'olawe, Lana'i and Ni'ihau? From a greenery standpoint, they have the geographical misfortune of having low elevations and of being in the lee of higher islands. Kaho'olawe at 1,483 feet and Lana'i at 3,370, lie downwind of Maui's Haleakala at 10,023 feet, West Maui's Pu'ukukui at 5,788, and Moloka'i's Kamakou at 4,961. And Ni'ihau's Pani'au at 1,281 feet lies in the lee of Kaua'i, whose peak at Kawaikini rises 5,243 feet.

Once the trade winds have dumped their rain on the windward islands, there is little left for the leewards. The remaining clouds often scud right over the smaller islands, sparing them nary a drop.

Thus, while the bigger windward islands have greenery galore and have year-round streams, Kaho'olawe, Lana'i and Ni'ihau have not a single perennial stream among them. For their drinking water, residents of Lana'i depend on a deep well that angles into the heart of the Island, and Ni'ihau's community of less than 300 people uses catchment systems and shallow wells. Kaho'olawe supports no full-time residential presence.

THE ISLANDS' VALLEYS

The windward sides of the larger islands sport yawning chasms of valleys. Some are deep and wide, like Waipi'o in the Kohala Mountains, whose legendary waterfall, Hi'ilawe, hangs threadlike from its green back wall. Some of the windward valleys are so narrow, like Awa'awapuhi on Kaua'i's Na Pali coastline, that stones falling from either side wall can strike you as you stand by the stream. The boulders around you there are marked gray-white by the impact of basalt on basalt.

Not all of the valley floors end up at sea level. Those that do not are called hanging valleys. On Kaua'i's Na Pali coast, Hanakoa is one. Awa'awapuhi is another. If you paddle a kayak along the cliffs at the base of these valleys, you can look up a steep rock face to where the greenery of the valley floor ends. These valleys' streams end in waterfalls, which are sometimes caught by the strong coastal updrafts and twisted into sheets of spray—cool showers for weary paddlers.

In ancient times, much of the travel between the valleys of the windward sides was likely done by canoe. Certainly most of the freight was carried this way. Trail building was a challenging task on these nearly vertical faces. Hawaiian roadbuilders took advantage of natural dikes and outcroppings. They built stone walls to support sections of trail where the terrain was too steep and rocky to excavate. They used natural thoroughfares like ridgetops and dropped into streambeds where necessary.

The Kalalau Trail on Kaua'i's Na Pali coast is such a path. In its first two miles from Ke'e Beach to Hanakapi'ai Beach, it rises hundreds of feet from sea level and drops again to sea level. From Hanakapi'ai, it zigzags up the face of the valley's west wall, then cruises in and out of valley after valley, so that at one moment a hiker stands looking straight down at the sea from the end of a ridge and minutes later is walking deep in vegetation under a dense canopy of trees, unable to see more than a few feet through the leaves. The trail spans one stream after another and, finally, 11 miles and several hours from Ke'e, the walker steps clear onto an eroded slope and looks down into Kalalau.

Like Waipi'o at the other end of the populated Hawaiian chain, Kalalau is a huge valley—wide, rugged, with an expanse of valley floor, and 2,000-foot cliffs marching along its sides and back. It is part of the State of Hawai'i's Na Pali Coast State Park and is one of the most popular backcountry camping spots in the Islands.

Kalalau features a white-sand beach, coastal Hawaiian agricultural terraces and other archaeological sites, sand-floored shoreline caves for camping, a running stream and a shoreline waterfall for showers. And that's all within the first 100 feet or so from the shorebreak. The valley is more than a mile deep, with trails for exploration, pools in the stream for swimming, fruit trees for snacks.

Most visitors discuss Kalalau in quiet voices that speak of awe. For many, visits here are like religious experiences. The crenellated clifftops, the fractal valley walls, the long, plunging waterfalls all combine to make this valley, like many of the other windward valleys, something bigger than life.

Steep cliff faces are visible at Honopu Beach and valley on Kaua'i's Na Pali coastline, where a sand dune is tucked into a protected corner.

Only a few wisps of cloud are visible on a calm day over Kaua'i's Kalalau Valley.

Wind and water erosion create remarkable, steep cliff faces, particularly on the windward sides of the Islands, as here on Windward O'ahu's Ko'olau Range.

Pale yellow-green kukui trees climb up
the narrow valleys of Kaua'i's Na Pali.

The drier habitat of Kaua'i's Waimea Canyon displays the effects of severe, constant erosion.

At Haleakala, Maui, the dust and cinder are swept into graceful patterns by wind and rain. A narrow ride ends in a rock spire.

A boat cruises near the Kalalau Valley shoreline, fronting the hanging valley, Nakeikiana'i'iwi.

The stream in Honopu Valley on Kaua'i cuts through the landslide rubble at the base of the cliffs.

The broad floor of Oʻahu's Makua Valley opens onto a leeward coast, where there is less rainfall and wind erosion, so hills tend not to be as steep as on windward coasts.

The name of the Lanipo Trail in Oʻahu's Koʻolau Mountains means "dense," referring to the thick vegetation at its summit.

ISLANDS AND OCEANS

That narrow zone where the sea and the land meet is a place for only the hardiest species, ones with one metaphorical and sometimes an actual foot in each.

Found here are plants that can survive despite occasional drenchings with salt spray, ones with specialized systems to keep them from drying out as salt crystals try to suck the moisture from the leaves and stems and as the sun beats down on them. It's a special place in Hawai'i, because it's one where the Hawaiian species evolved for this kind of location have an advantage over many of the introduced plants that have gained Hawai'i footholds.

You find these plants hanging precariously from cracks on rock faces, just beyond the wash of the waves. You may find them inside the sea arches that form when the surf eats away at weaknesses in the rock, leaving the harder rock to form natural bridges.

You find animal life here, too. Paddle an outrigger canoe along the rocky coastlines of the Islands, and you will find places stained with guano. Here, seabirds roost just a wing and a breeze from their food source—the sea. Some seabirds lay their eggs and hatch their young on narrow rock ledges. The young birds

The constant action of the sea has cut a hole in this ridge jutting out into the Pacific off Moloka'i's northern coast, as viewed from Haka'a'ano.

are left to hang on as the ocean winds whip into, and around, their tiny footholds.

Walk into a shallow sea cave and the compact Hawaiian noddies or *noio*, with their dark bodies and powder-white foreheads, will sweep out of their roosts, dive-bombing to protest your intrusion. They feed near shore, and will often head out of their nesting areas in flocks when they detect a school of small fish nearby.

Forms of shoreline life on the main Hawaiian islands are protected by their harsh environment and by the tough terrain. Better protection still is afforded to those plants and birds that use the little islands separated by patches of ocean from the main islands.

The American naturalist Aldo Leopold once wrote that the best remaining examples of the plant life of the American prairies were contained in the narrow sections of grass alongside the railroad tracks. They'd been fenced and thus protected from intensive cattle grazing and from the farmers' plows, and much of the ancient diversity of the American West could be found there a century after it was gone from most of the surrounding lands.

O'ahu's Ka'ena Point just westward into the Ka'ie'ie Waho Channel. Note the vigorous action of the waves on the windward side, to the left, and the much lighter surf to the leeward.

OFF-SHORE ISLAND TREASURES

In Hawai'i, small offshore islands and jagged coastal cliffs contain treasured bits of the Islands' natural heritage.

The State of Hawai'i recognizes 96 named minor islands off the eight major Hawaiian islands. A few, like Mokuolo'e or Coconut Island in Kane'ohe Bay, have been significantly developed, but the vast majority could not support human life and are difficult to access, so are left alone. Most of the rocks and islets off the coastlines of the Islands are now wildlife refuges, and for good reason. They are the places where bulldozer treads have never left tracks, where well-meaning gardeners have not planted pretty alien plants,

where homeowners haven't built, developers haven't excavated, and where cats and rats and mongooses and feral dogs haven't found a haven.

Thus, the native plants of these Islands, while often facing a stormy, salty, difficult life, have not had to face a great deal of competition and disruption that wasn't a part of Hawai'i's life before the first humans arrived. And the native birds have been able to nest in relative peace.

OFF-SHORE ISLAND BIRDS

Atop Mokuho'oniki, a hump-backed island off the east end of Moloka'i, the land is a Swiss cheese of burrows of the wedge-tailed shearwater, whose parents arrive each spring to take up residence in these small caves, no wider than a rolled-up Sunday newspaper, and often not much deeper than the newspaper is long. Eggs are laid, and the chicks hatch, normally one per pair, and the parents take turns going out to sea for food, which is brought back and regurgitated for the chick. By the late fall, the chicks are fatter than their parents, though still covered with the fuzz of young birds. The adult shearwaters stop feeding them and fly off. In the subsequent days and weeks, the chicks lose their fuzz and grow mature feathers, and lose their baby fat. One day, when they are hungry enough and their wings are ready, they begin stepping out of the burrows and spreading their wings, feeling the lift of the wind. Ultimately, generally around November, they may take a few steps, spread their wings, soar off and head out over the deep ocean, generally not to return until they are ready to begin raising their own young.

The wedge-tailed shearwaters and other birds of Mokuho'oniki off Moloka'i, of Moku'ae'ae off north Kaua'i, and of the small islands throughout the Hawaiian chain, have several distinct advantages over their relatives who nest on the main islands.

Dark-rumped petrels that nest in deep caves atop Haleakala have suffered severe predation by mongooses, which can engage in a kind of killing frenzy, entering one cave after another, slaughtering the helpless nestlings. They kill far more than they could possibly eat.

The Newell's shearwaters of Kaua'i, which nest in inland burrow colonies, suffer similar problems with cats and dogs.

MAIN ISLAND BIRDS

Main island birds have another problem. Many species leave their nests, taking their first flights, just after dark. Perhaps they are attracted by the sheen of the starlight off the ocean, and perhaps this directs them down the mountainsides and out to sea. But these days, there are obstacles along the way.

The birds fly low and, depending on the location of their burrow communities, they sometimes fly down to the sea entirely over land and sometimes follow river valleys on their way to the ocean. Almost inevitably, they come across power lines strung along highways or strung over bridges. Many each year hit the power lines, are stunned or injured and fall to the ground, where they can become prey to feral animals and pets, or are killed by cars. They have difficulty taking flight from flat ground, and generally are stuck unless someone comes along to help.

The birds also are attracted to lights. Street lights, stadium lights, hotel lights over the water—these all divert the fledglings from their journey. Fans at November football games on Kaua'i sometimes see shearwaters flying in great circles around the stadium lights, swooping round and round, until they hit something or fall to the ground in exhaustion.

RESCUE PROGRAMS

During the past two decades, officials on Kaua'i, O'ahu and Maui have set up rescue programs for the shearwa-

Huelo Island stands narrow and tall off Moloka'i's northern coast, its summit carpeted with a stand of the native loulu palm, which once was a dominant forest tree but is now uncommon.

ters, petrels and other birds that get into trouble with the lights over developed Hawai'i. More than 1,000 birds each year are recovered by Good Samaritans on Kaua'i alone. They are checked for injuries and, if healthy, are released from windy shoreline areas, where they can immediately spread those wide wings and take flight.

Scientists do not know whether the rescued birds ultimately survive as well as their relatives who never fall into human hands, but, clearly, those birds that never have to face power lines and electric lights stand a better chance of survival.

Bird experts in the case of Kaohikaipu, a small island off Makapu'u, O'ahu, are trying to use its relative isolation to create a safe haven. The researchers noted that Laysan albatrosses, once residents of the main islands but long missing here, have started returning. There were no predacious mammals when albatrosses lived here thousands of years ago. But today, they readily become prey, primarily for feral dogs. Scientists have gone to Kaohikaipu with fake eggs and dummy birds, and have started playing recordings of albatross calls. The goal is to convince young albatrosses that there's a colony here and that they should nest there. Albatrosses nesting for the first time face extreme danger on O'ahu, but, if the birds select the islet as a nesting place, they'll continue to return year after year, and it should help protect them and their offspring.

THE EXPLOITATION OF OFF-SHORE ISLANDS

Being on an offshore islet isn't always a guarantee of safety, though. Some of these islands have been inhabited by rats, which prey on the birds. Early European explorers left rabbits on some offshore islands to provide food for sailors who might be shipwrecked there in the future. The rabbits reproduced, ate much of the vegetation, which in turn caused erosion, making unstable or unusable some traditional seabird nesting sites. On some of O'ahu's offshore islands, residents visit with family pets, which can kill off many young birds in a short time. And simply having people on the island can cause damage. A 150-pound person stepping on a shearwater burrow can easily collapse it, potentially injuring, killing or trapping the fledgling inside. Hawai'i anglers once protested the Navy's bombing of the little island of Ka'ula, 21 miles from Ni'ihau, because the bombs damaged seabird nesting sites, and the anglers depended on the seabirds to help them find schools of fish.

ISLAND NOMENCLATURE

Some of these islands have names that give them special character.

Ka'ula reportedly got its name from a bird, but the story about the specific bird and how it gave its name to the island is lost. Legends tell of a shark god that lived at Ka'ula, and anglers today complain that sharks are so plentiful in the area that they often cannot get a hooked fish to the surface in one piece.

The island off the Mokapu peninsula of O'ahu is appropriately called Mokumanu, or Bird Island.

Mokoli'i is an island in Kane'ohe Bay and commonly known in recent years as Chinaman's Hat, probably because its shape reminded viewers of the headgear worn by Chinese laborers in the rice and taro fields around the bay. But its Hawaiian name has more poetic meanings. One refers to a battle between the Hawaiian demigoddess Hi'iaka, who fought with a lizard, Mokoli'i. She defeated the lizard, and Mokoli'i island is said to be the tail of the lizard, while a nearby lowland portion of O'ahu is its body. Another tale describes Mokoli'i as a demon who is broken into pieces in a fight with the hero Kaulu. The island is one of the pieces of the demon. Incidentally, although Mokoli'i has the appearance of a small volcano, it isn't. It is a formation known as a sea stack, a piece of land that was formerly part of the island, but which has been separated from the main island by erosion.

Off Hana, Maui, is the island Mokuhano, meaning "Majestic Island," perhaps for its appearance. And in Hilo Bay is Mokuola, "Healing Island," for a spring there that was known for its medicinal qualities. This island is now better known as Hilo's Coconut Island.

An island off the north coast of Moloka'i, Huelo, is a museum of Hawaiian natural history. There are only three acres, but it is heavily forested with native fan palms, *loulu*, while few are found on the main island. Pollen records indicate that Hawai'i's only native palm genus, Pritchardia, was once a dominant member of the Islands' lowland forests. But rats eating the seeds and agricultural clearing probably played major parts in its dramatic decline. The fan palms of Huelo form as dense a stand as you are likely to find anywhere in the State. There are traditions that indicate the palm played an important role in the recreation of the early Hawaiians. One story says the palm leaves were woven into hammocks, from which people were tossed into the ocean. Another talks of people using the fan palm leaves as parachutes or hang gliders when they jumped into the sea from high outcroppings. The leaves are too small to have kept anyone aloft, but they might have slowed their fall enough to avoid injury or gained enough lateral distance to get beyond a rock ledge.

Manana or Rabbit Island is viewed from offshore, with O'ahu in the background.

The Holei Sea Arch at Hawai'i Volcanoes National Park shows where the sea has cut away softer rock, leaving an arch of hard basalt.

Hawaiian sailing canoes at anchor in front of Mokoli'i, whose unique configuration suggests it is a cinder cone. Actually, it is a sea stack, separated from nearby O'ahu through the forces of erosion.

On North Moloka'i, some of the world's highest sea cliffs are separated by wide, deep valleys.

In the waters off Maui, the crescent tuff cone island of Molokini attracts tourists seeking to dive in its clear waters.

A stream flows from a waterfall on one side of the arch at Honopu Valley on Kaua'i's Na Pali Coast and travels through the arch to reach the ocean on the other side.

The reefs of North O'ahu break up ocean swells and create areas of flat water favored by windsurfers.

The rain forest at Hawai'i
Volcanoes National Park
in Kilauea, Hawai'i is a
complex ecosystem. The
most common overstory
tree is the *'ohi'a,* which
protects a range of species
of ferns, vines and shrubs
growing below.

A sisal, a plant originally brought to
Hawai'i for its tough fibers, grows wild at
Pelekunu Valley on the north shore of
Moloka'i.

RAIN FORESTS
AND VEGETATION

The lowlands and middle elevations of the main Hawaiian Islands are largely vegetated with plants alien to Hawai'i. Some—like the coconut, sugar cane, taro, *kukui* trees and *ti* plants—were brought by the early Polynesian immigrants. More came with later visitors. If you look around you anywhere outside the highlands and rain forests of Hawai'i, you're likely to be seeing alien species.

The shower trees, java plum, mango, lychee, eucalyptus, all pines, papaya, and guava are all imports. In your garden, most of the vegetables are imports. Among your flowers, do you have roses, peonies, anthuriums, heliconias? Imports. There are some native species of hibiscus, but the common red hibiscus was brought in. Its scientific name translates to "Rose of China." And virtually all the fancy hibiscus flowers you'll find in Hawai'i yards are products of horticultural interbreeding. Your houseplants are most likely aliens, and so are most of the grasses in your lawn.

HAWAI'I'S NATIVE TREES

To find a largely native ecosystem, you generally need to go *mauka*, into the highlands. Hawai'i's wet forests, largely because people haven't spent much time there, are some of the most precious of Hawai'i's natural areas.

Here, you find the rich diversity of the native plant life, and if you have a good eye, the diversity of insect and bird life as well.

For example, at Kilauea—around the Hawai'i Volcanoes National Park—the forests are dense with species.

Overhead, you will find the dominant tree of the Hawaiian forest, the *'ohi'a*. This ruggedly attractive member of the myrtle family has stiff, dark-green leaves, a scaling pale bark, and flowers that are a spray of stamens, giving them the appearance of a small fireworks skyburst. The flowers are generally red, but a few trees have orange, salmon or even yellow or white blooms. Some residents refer to the tree as *'ohi'a* and the blossoms as *lehua*. Others use the names interchangeably. The red Hawaiian forest bird known as the *'i'iwi*, which has a long, curved beak, often can be seen feeding at the blossoms. The flowers and leaf buds make attractive lei, but there is a Hawaiian tradition that if you pick the *lehua*, you must pick it only on your way out of the forest. To pick it on your way in is to invite rain.

Other popular trees of the forest include the *koa*, a majestic species, whose wood is prized for furniture and decorative carpentry, and the *'olapa*, whose leaves flutter in the slightest breeze.

Beneath the canopy stand the tree ferns, *hapu'u*, whose trunks can grow to 16 feet, and whose long fronds stretch out in all directions. The fern trunks, masses of matted roots, are prized by orchid growers and other gardeners for support of their plants, are also seedbeds for native

Hapu'u tree fern fronds grow out of fresh lavas at Kilauea Iki in Hawai'i Volcanoes National Park in Kilauea, Hawai'i.

species. Often, a number of seedlings can be seen growing out of the trunks of *hapu'u*.

Still closer to the forest floor is an incredible diversity of plants. You find the succulent native peperomia, *'ala'alawainui*, whose leaf when chewed leaves a refreshing minty flavor in the mouth. And the tasty red-berried *'ohelo*. And any number of mosses and low ferns. And much more.

But even in the rain forest, all's not well. A devastating insect, the two-spotted leafhopper, is severely damaging *'ohi'a* trees. The aggressive vine known as banana poka smothers *koa* forests. Feral pigs knock down *hapu'u* to eat its starchy core. An imported ornamental called miconia, with huge solid leaves, forms dense stands and can shade out virtually all native plants where it grows.

The State of Hawai'i, with the help of the federal government and private conservation groups like The Nature Conservancy of Hawai'i, is attempting to control the arrival of new species that threaten Hawai'i's natives, but the job is a tough one.

THE ARRIVAL OF NON-NATIVE PLANTS

In pre-human Hawai'i, new plants and animals had a tough time arriving. They had to cross more than 2,000 miles of ocean from any direction. They had to land somewhere that suited their requirements, and they had to be able to reproduce. Few species arrived and they filled the available ecological spots by evolving—this cousin taking to the wet country, that one to the dry, this one to shady areas and that one to full sun. Animal life evolved, too. This bird developed a deeply curved bill that let it get into the curved blossom of a particular lobelia plant. Another bird may have developed a short, tough bill good for cracking certain seeds. Still another developed a bill that let it probe into tree bark looking for insects. And among insects, ones like the Hawaiian vinegar fly evolved into hundreds of different species, each filling a specific niche.

Few mammals could make the trip from distant continents, and Hawai'i ended up with only two native mammals that survive today—the Hawaiian bat, which could fly here, and the Hawaiian monk seal, which could swim.

It was bad enough for the native species that humans brought things from elsewhere, which ended up competing with the natives. Hawaiians brought chickens, which, once some got away, competed with native flightless ground birds, of which there were many. Both Hawaiians and Europeans brought rats, which went after native plants as well as native birds and other species. Sugar planters brought in mongooses to chase the rats, but they, too, took a liking to birds. Someone imported the African snail, which can be used to make the delicacy escargot, but it became a serious agricultural pest. So, a couple of species of cannibal snails were imported, and they quickly began attacking Hawai'i's remarkable native tree snails. Today, the entire genus of wonderfully varied O'ahu tree snails is on the endangered species list. These snail shells were so attractive that they were actively collected and even worn as jewelry.

INSECTS AND HAZARDOUS PESTS

But the purposefully imported creatures aren't the only problem. Every year, many new insects and other pests arrive in Hawai'i by accident. Not all of them become established, but some do. It is far easier today than in pre-human Hawai'i for a newcomer to get here.

They come the same way humans and their belongings do. By plane, by ship, through the mail, in shipping containers. As many as a dozen insect pests each year come into Hawai'i. One of the most frightening ones in recent years is the two-spotted leafhopper. In addition to attacking the *'ohi'a* trees, this tiny plant attacks more than 300 other forms of plant life, including several extremely rare native trees. It hits commercial plants like taro or *kalo* and ornamental species, as well. No one brought it in here on purpose. It appears to be well controlled by natural enemies in its native Asia, but it arrived in Hawai'i having left its enemies behind. Researchers have gone to China to look for the leafhopper and pests they might import to control it, but it is so rare there that the work is time consuming and difficult.

There are so many potentially hazardous pests in the world that it's tough to identify specific ones you really want to keep out. But one such is the brown tree snake, which arrived on Guam to silence the forest and so effectively killed off the birdlife. It also went after insects, lizards, and has been found attacking human babies.

The snake could readily silence what's left of Hawai'i's native forest bird population and, since some of them are responsible for the pollination of native plants, the high forests of Hawai'i could suffer dramatically.

IMPORTED PLANTS

At elevations lower than those of the high wet forests, the vegetation changes from mainly Hawaiian species to more alien species, and from wetland plants to those better adapted to drier conditions.

There is plenty of Hawaiian history in the imported plants of the Islands. Many were brought in by people who hoped to establish agricultural industries here. The sisal, whose fibers are used to make natural cordage, still grows wild around the drier parts of the Islands, though no surviving industry developed.

Deep in many valleys, you can find dense stands of coffee, remnants of planters' efforts, long abandoned. Ironically, those wild coffee communities create problems for efforts to expand Hawai'i's modern coffee industry, since they harbor fruit flies. The fruit flies provide a steady source of new pests, so that no amount of insect control on the commercial plantations alone can wipe them out.

In Hawai'i's back country, you can find tobacco, indigo, and many other formerly commercial crops that have now gone wild.

Most of the palms that grow around Hawai'i are imports. And even among the Pritchardia, the genus of Hawai'i's only native palms, the most popular species for landscape work is an imported one.

LOWLAND NATIVE PLANTS

There are still a few examples of lowland native plants, and a few of them are found in stands where a group of native species survive together. They tend to be in areas which, for one reason or another, have been protected from development and feral animals. One such area is on the island of Lana'i, where a ranch manager who valued natural history recognized a cluster of native plants and put a fence around them to protect them from the cattle. The area is now a preserve overseen by The Nature Conservancy of Hawai'i.

A team of plant finders from the National Tropical Botanical Garden has found many rare Hawaiian species by searching vertical cliff faces—areas so steep that even goats can't get there. Steve Perlman and Ken Wood dangle from ropes, collecting samples and pollinating plants whose natural pollinators, whether birds or insects, have themselves become rare or extinct. They try to bring seeds of some of those plants back to the National Tropical Botanical Garden nursery to provide a species safety net. If a storm or landslide, or a particularly sure-footed goat, were to kill off the last of the species in the wild, the nursery specimens could be used to reestablish the plants in the wild. It is a technique that has already been put into practice more than once.

Tourists crowd to view the remarkable vegetation of the Fern Grotto along Kaua'i's Wailua River.

Introduced Kahili Ginger sports spectacular, fragrant flowers, but is an aggressive intruder in the native forest, where its roots form dense mats that exclude all native plants.

The rainy Puna coastline of the Big Island features seaweeds on the coastal rocks and a forest growing right down to the shore.

Native Hawaiians filled many wet valley floors with their staple crop, *kalo* or taro.

Hawai'i's native forests create superb watersheds, soaking up rains and releasing the moisture slowly into mountain streams, which run even during extended dry weather.

A jacaranda tree fills the scene with its blue blossoms in Upcountry Maui.

Orchids bloom at a Maui nursery, with the West Maui Mountains in the background.

Red jade vines flower at Nani Mau Gardens, Hilo.

A stream plunges, then plunges again deep in Hanalei Valley, Kaua'i, creating a scenic view for passengers on a tour helicopter.

WATERFALLS, RIVERS & STREAMS

Falling water catches the imagination. It's powerful or fragile, thundering or whispering, sometimes even disappearing.

Hawai'i is blessed with innumerable waterfalls. They thrill visitors and are well represented in Hawaiian song. People jump over them, bathe in them, watch them for hours.

The names are the poetry of Hawai'i. 'Akaka Falls, Waimea Falls, Hi'ilawe, Wailele, Wailua and Manoa are ones that come to mind.

The highest waterfall that cascades down a cliffside is Moloka'i's Kahiwa, which most of the year is a thin, white thread against the Island's green northern cliffs. Kahiwa travels 1,000 feet horizontally as it drops 1,750 feet.

The Big Island's 'Akaka Falls, with a 442-foot drop, is the tallest when you count straight-line fall.

We cite these heights, but the figures are notoriously inaccurate. Often, they are estimates made decades or a century or more ago, which have never since been checked. The heights of tall waterfalls can be tough to measure.

WAILUA FALLS

Wailua Falls on Kaua'i has long been listed in the State's statistical charts at 80 feet. A number of people have jumped from the Wailua Falls, and many of them have died as a result of the impact with the water. Ultimately, an accurate measurement found it to be 200 feet high.

Wailua Falls displays a feature that is characteristic of many sheer drop falls. The river immediately above the waterfall runs over a thick, particularly solid lava flow, which has prevented the river level from sloping gradually toward the sea. Instead, as the water reaches the edge of the flow, it drops precipitously. The softer rock below the big flow is steadily worn away by the constant flow of water, until it undercuts the big lava flow. Eventually, the lip of the old lava flow, no longer supported from below, collapses. The waterfall thus steadily creeps back toward the water's source.

Kaua'i's Wailua Falls has a stream running over a dense, thick lava flow, while softer lavas below are undercutting.

This is not a feature unique to Hawai'i's waterfalls. Even the famed Niagara Falls has been moving steadily upstream for eons.

PLUNGE POOLS

Many of Hawai'i's taller waterfalls feature plunge pools. The streams flow over layers of hard rock, as at Wailua, then drop into small pools, which are often quite deep. The water travels along the next hard layer and plunges again over the side.

The area Kaua'i helicopter pilots know as the Wai'ale'ale Crater drains the wettest spot on earth. Its steep cliff face features dozens of waterfalls most of the time, which multiply in rainy weather to the point of being uncountable.

BOOM AND BUST CYCLES

In drier parts of the island, intermittent streams feature boom and bust cycles. For long periods they may have no water at all, but, after a heavy rain, they can feature flash floods and a violence that rips up trees and changes the valley floor landscape. Their waterfalls are given to muddy displays and rolling boulders that often burst on impact against the rocks below. Whether a stream is dry or running, Hawai'i's narrow valleys are subject to flash flooding, and it's wise to remain on high ground when the rains are falling heavily upstream.

The sound of the onrushing water can seem like that of a big wind, and a hiker or camper waiting by the streambed for the breeze to come around the corner can face serious danger.

Some valleys formed by the falling water often have winds blowing upstream. As a result, smaller waterfalls can be blown into tiny droplets, the fresh winds blowing mists back up the mountainsides. There is a waterfall in Nu'uanu Valley on O'ahu, commonly called Upside-down Falls. Its Hawaiian name, Waipuhia, means "Blown Water."

When the mists catch the sunlight, rainbows form. Hawai'i Island's Rainbow Falls has the same Hawaiian name—Waianuenue, "Rainbow Water."

Waterfalls also create mists when they crash into the rocks or pool at their bases. This can create a microclimate of extreme moisture all around the base of the waterfall, and forms a favorite spot for fern and moss growth.

A few of Hawai'i's streams end with a vertical drop directly into the ocean. There is a sea cave along Kaua'i's Na Pali coastline where swimmers and boaters can position themselves directly under the falling water, a refreshing treat.

Rainbow Falls near Hilo drops into a turbulent pool, shaded by giant monstera leaves and the red flowers of an African tulip tree.

The strong flow and hearty mists of the Big Island's Akaka Falls provide plenty of moisture for dense vegetation even on the steep cliff faces around it.

A Waipio Valley waterfall cascades through a rainbow into a plunge pool.

Native shrimps and gobies abound in the small streams of Hawaiian mountains. The gobies have fins fused into small suction cups that help them climb up wet rock faces to get over small waterfalls.

The 'Iao Needle stands high above the splash of 'Iao Valley's stream, at Wailuku, Maui.

The Wailua River below Wailua Falls is near sea level and flows quietly toward the shore.

Waterfalls drop into successive plunge pools on the nearly vertical face of Waimanu Valley, in Hawai'i's Kohala Mountains.

Numerous sea stacks form small islands off Moloka'i's north shore.

ROCKY COASTS & BEACHES

It's no surprise that activity in Hawai'i is centers around the shoreline. This is the heart of Hawai'i. The coastline defines islands. And it is one of the key reasons many people live here.

The coast is a place where a living can be made, whether with a thrownet or at a hotel job. It's a place where the mind is calmed, whether through reading a book in a beach chair or meditating to the sound of the waves. It's a place of activity—surfing, canoeing, swimming, snorkeling or deep diving, sailing, wading, sunbathing, fishing, beachcombing, and so much more.

Hawai'i, though one of the smallest of the states, has by virtue of being a chain of islands more coastline than many states that have substantially larger land areas. The Hawai'i Data Book reports that Hawai'i has some 750 miles of coastline, based on a general outline of each island.

And, if you follow each inlet in and out, the figure stretches to more than 1,000 miles. And, since under State law all land seaward of the high-water mark or vegetation line is State property, it's virtually all technically available to the public.

WHITE SAND BEACHES

To the uninitiated, and to the tourist industry, white-sand beaches are the most valuable. Virtually every hotel in Hawai'i is on one. But they hardly represent the whole story when it comes to Hawai'i's shorelines.

Many think only white sand when they think of sandy beaches, but Hawai'i has beaches of many colors.

The white-sand beach is made up largely of bits of coral, but also of pieces of shells. On some beaches the pieces are large, and these coastline areas are favored by people collecting shells, since such beaches, often inland of extensive reefs, frequently contain whole shells washed up off the reef surface. Beaches fronting wide, open bays often have finer sands.

White sand is produced by boulders grinding on coral and by shells and larger pieces of coral smashing into each other in the surf. But one of the other sources of fine coral sand is the parrot fish, which uses powerful teeth to bite off pieces of live coral. Divers can sometimes see a parrot fish swimming and trailing a thin line of new sand as it defecates.

BLACK SAND BEACHES

In areas where fresh lava is pouring into the ocean, the beaches may be black. This is because the orange molten lava hits the sea, instantly cools and shatters into tiny, shiny black shards, which wash back up on the shoreline to form glistening beaches. Even after the lava flow has stopped, black sand can continue to form, as the young black rocks bash into each other in the surf. Eventually, coral begins growing on the new bottom, and the black sands are supplanted by white.

There are a few sand beaches in Hawai'i with a distinctly greenish tint. This comes from the green olivine crystals that are common in some lavas. A beachgoer can pick up a handful of sand and readily separate the green grains.

Gray and brown beaches sometimes form at the mouths of streams, where ancient, weathered boulders have rubbed together and created basalt sand. Since many of those boulders also contain olivine, such beaches also can have a greenish hue.

A shoreline plateau in the foreground juts out from the cliffs of Moloka'i's north coast.

ROCKY SHORES

Much of Hawai'i's shore is not sandy beach, but is rugged and inhospitable rock. At first, it might not be apparently available for use by humans. To think that, however, would be a mistake. Even the roughest, rockiest, least hospitable shores are important to Hawai'i and its people. Some cliffsides drop directly into deep water, but they are used.

'Opihi pickers clamber over such areas, slipping blades under the hardy limpets and dropping the delicacies into bags at their waists. It is dangerous work, and pickers are killed each year when unexpected surf smashes them and drags them into a churning sea. Divers below the surface check cracks and crevasses, looking for lobsters and fish seeking basalt protection. Along Kaua'i's Na Pali, which means "The Cliffs," there is a spot where a small waterfall drips down the rocks. It is called Waiku'auhoe, "Water of the Paddle Handle," because this was a place where fishing canoes would stop for refreshment of their crews. Paddlers would put their wooden paddles into the waterfall and let the water run down the handles into their mouths.

BOULDER BEACHES

Many coasts have boulder beaches, dangerous to walk on, difficult to get onto from the sea, and difficult to use for ocean access from the land. But a coast is a coast and often provided access to the sea, despite an inhospitable appearance. Early Hawaiian residents used what was available. On the Big Island, where sandy beaches are few, fishing communities built canoe ladders for launching their outrigger fishing canoes. The ladders are called that because that's how they looked—two long poles reaching from the dry land out into the water, with cross-pieces lashed on. Often, holes would be chipped into large shoreline rocks or into lava outcroppings. The holes would be used to tie down the fishing ladder poles. For launching, a crew might carry the canoe to the ladder, then slide it into the sea with a retreating wave. Returning would have been trickier, requiring exquisite timing of crew and steersman to put the nose of the canoe gently on the ladder so waiting hands could pull the canoe up.

TRAVEL BETWEEN COASTS

Canoes were used for much movement between valleys on the more rugged coastlines, but Hawaiians also used trails. They often took advantage of existing ledges. There is an interesting feature on the Na Pali cliff face between Nu'alolo, a hanging valley with a rock beach, and Nu'alolo Kai, a coastal flat with sections of sand beach. Nu'alolo had many taro patches, and Nu'alolo-kai held a fishing community. There had to be a way to get between them, but the cliff face here is very steep and no one ledge goes all the way along it. There is a spot where one ledge disappears, but another exists more than 10 feet below it. The lower ledge is tucked deeper into the cliff than the upper. To allow walkers to get from one to the other, early Hawaiians chipped two holes in the rock, as they did with canoe ladders, and lashed a ladder onto the cliff face. Some reports indicate the ladder was made of a palm trunk.

With such techniques, virtually every section of coastline was made available and traversible.

NEARSHORE WATERS

Even today, some residents who use the ocean to provide food refer to the nearshore waters as their refrigera-

The rough North Pacific swells have eaten away at the wet Hana, Maui, coastline, creating a jumble of cliffs, arches, peninsulas and sea stacks.

tors. The fish, mollusks, edible seaweeds and all the other edible marine life were there, fresh, for the taking. The former abundance of marine life is a thing of the past, but many Hawai'i residents still fish regularly for sport and to feed their families.

The nearshore marine community of Hawai'i has never had the volume of fish that are found in many temperate areas with extensive continental shelves. Hawai'i's ocean bottom drops off quickly into extreme depths. Within a few miles of any island's shore, the water can be a mile or two deep. The deep waters tend to be low in nutrients, limiting the amount of biomass that can be produced here. Without something similar to a continental shelf, there are not enough nutrients to support the huge fisheries of, say, the western coast of the United States. However, what Hawai'i lacks in volume of marine life it makes up for in diversity. The islands have far more species of nearshore marine life than many Mainland areas. There are more than 3,000 species of fishes, mollusks, seaweeds and other forms of marine life in the nearshore waters of the Islands.

High diversity and comparatively low numbers of individual species create a problem when fishing pressure is applied selectively. An active fishery in one species, such as lobster or the tasty fishes in the snapper family, can quickly deplete the target species' stocks. That has happened throughout the Islands, and both State and federal agencies are working on solutions. In some areas, notably the Northwestern Hawaiian Islands, commercial fishing is under strict federal control to protect fishery stocks.

HAWAI'I'S FRESHWATER LIFE

Even Hawai'i's freshwater forms of aquatic life have oceanic roots. Several of them spend part of their life, generally as plankton, in the Pacific. Since virtually every native creature that lives in the water had to have reached Hawai'i via the ocean, it's not surprising that some of them still recall their salt water pasts by spending part of their lives in the ocean. The native stream gobies, or *'o'opu*, come down to the mouths of streams each year and lay millions of eggs. The eggs hatch and the tiny fishes travel out into the ocean for the first part of their lives. They sweep and sway with the winds and currents, but eventually they return to the stream and river mouths and head upstream, to mature in fresh water and generally never to live in the sea again.

Several of Hawai'i's *'o'opu* have evolved specially for their lives in small, rough island streams. The fins on their undersides have joined to form a feature that acts like a suction cup. The fishes can use it to hold themselves to rock faces during flash floods, and they can use them to wriggle up the vertical faces of waterfalls. As a result, *'o'opu* are found even high up the most rugged streams in the State.

AN ARRAY OF HABITATS

There is a surprising array of habitats even within a few feet of the wash of the waves. Deepwater fishes may swim just a few feet from shore at the base of cliffs that drop directly into the sea.

Nearshore reefs support other species and generally smaller fishes. Coral reefs create complex habitats that can support a great variety of species. Some of these will be invisible to the casual observer. Eel, lobster and octopus are animals that remain hiding in shelter most of the time and often come into the open only when they are actively hunting, often only at night. Many of the fishes of this zone are very colorful, like the parrot fishes, Moorish idols and butterfly fishes. Powerful predators like the jacks, or *ulua*, which can grow to more than 100 pounds, also cruise the nearshore waters. They often attack prey right in the breaking surf.

Waterworn boulders and distant waterfalls mark the shoreline at Waipio'o, Hawai'i.

A sand beach may appear devoid of life, but this is an illusion. Crabs burrow in the sand. Several kinds of shells exist just below the surface. Fishes can hide in shallow sandy areas, simply diving into the sand and allowing it to cover them, effectively hiding them from predators.

There are species adapted to surviving even the most powerful breaking surf on rock shorelines. The *'opihi* is one. So are several kinds of sea urchins and a range of tough seaweeds and hard algae.

TIDEPOOLS

Tidepools provide what appears at first to be a placid habitat. But most tidepools are filled by regular infusions of salt water from breaking surf. The species that live there must be tough. They need to be able to survive the pounding of the sea. They must also be able to handle dramatic water temperature changes, since fairly small pools may be subjected to harsh sun that can heat them to bathwater temperatures. They need to be able to survive marked changes in salinity as well, either from rainfall turning the water brackish or several days or weeks of evaporation turning it extremely salty. Tidepools can be home to many kinds of shells, and are particularly popular with hermit crabs, which inhabit shells whose original occupants have died. Specialized seaweeds live here, as well as sea cucumbers and many small fishes. Gobies, which have the capacity to jerk their bodies aggressively and thus to hop from pond to pond, are common inhabitants.

There is life even high on the shoreline, in places where only the salt spray normally goes. Most have the colors of the rocks on which they live, like the gray and black shells such as the *pupu kolea* and the *pipipi*, and black *'a'ama* crabs.

Mankind's effect on these valuable life forms is significant. Care must be taken to preserve nature and not adversely affect delicate ecological balances.

The coastal pools at Ka'upulehu, on the lavas of an 1801 lava flow, form a habitat for the immature forms of many Island fish species.

Kaua'i's Na Pali, which means "the cliffs," also features deep valleys and white sand beaches, all enclosed in the Na Pali Coast State Park, a favorite of hikers, campers and kayakers.

A green-sand beach, rich in olivine, forms at South Point, Hawai'i.

Moloka'i's Papohaku Beach faces west and was once the site of a mining operation that provided O'ahu's construction industry with sand.

Rough surf at Keʻe, Kauaʻi, is broken up by a nearshore reef.

Clouds sit atop each peak *mauka* of Kailua on Oʻahu.

Waterworn basalt boulders and rough rocky outcroppings form the shore at Ke'anae, Maui.

The native *hala* trees that populated the shore at Lumaha'i, Kaua'i, now compete with introduced ironwoods.

Kailua Beach on O'ahu is one of the state's most popular recreation spots.

A black rock beach runs under a rock arch along Maui's Hana coastline.

The white sands of Mo'omomi, Moloka'i, are blown by the wind to form the sand dunes in the background.

Kilauea Point, Kaua'i, the site of the northernmost lighthouse in the main Hawaiian Islands, is a seabird nesting site and national wildlife refuge.

A surfer catches a wave at Hanalei Bay, Kaua'i.

Islands off Lanikai, O'ahu, lie across a stretch of shallow water from the sandy shore.

A breaking wave forms a perfect tube at Waimea Bay, O'ahu.

South Kaua'i's Spouting Horn is formed by a rocky plateau lava tube that redirects the power of waves upward.

The Waimea surf regularly rolls far inland, causing erosion of coastal properties, although some buildings, such as structures in the background, are safely situated on high ground.

Waves crash at sunset on the reefs and shoreline cliffs at Keʻe, Kauaʻi.

SUNSET & SUNRISE

Conversation stops for sunsets. There may be a few "oohs" and "aahs," but when we're aware of sunsets, when we have a view of the sun's dropping below the horizon, most of us stop and take a moment to ourselves. There's something seminal about this celestial event and, even though it occurs daily, we don't tire of it.

Going to watch sunsets is a thing for friends, a thing for people alone, for lovers and for people grieving. We are creatures of light, and it takes a certain act of faith not to panic when our planet turns its other side to the sun...faith that the light will return, faith that a new day will come, that things will be better.

We are often fatigued at sunset—from a day's work, or a day's play. Sunrise is different. Most of us never see it. We see the light in the sky and know it's there. Our faith has been repaid, but we take the sunrise for granted. We are going about our business, getting ready for the day. Most of us will watch far more sunsets in our lives than sunrises.

Hawai'i's best-known sunrise is the one over Haleakala. You must rise in the deep of the night, at a time when body temperature is at its coolest and getting out of bed is hardest. You brew up the coffee, take a cup and pour the rest in a thermos. And, in the darkness, you drive up the winding road to the summit of Maui's tallest mountain. There, alongside a parking lot, or on a cinder hill, you wait for the faint glow, then the gradual brightening of black sky to gray and, finally, to pale blue. The stars creep back out of the visible sky. And then it's there, heralded by beams of light. Casting shadows across the summit caldera. Rising until its full circumference is visible, and then slowly bringing light to the rest of the Island. High on the mountaintop, you have seen it before anyone else on the Island, but now its rays ignite the treetops, illuminate the ridges, and slowly begin to fill the valleys. The birds are calling. House lights flick on. The day has begun.

During much of the year, the sun rises south of Hawai'i, but twice each year it rises directly east of us and passes directly overhead. Flagpole shadows disappear in the middle of this day, which astronomers have named "Lahaina Noon." It happens twice at any given spot in Hawai'i, once about a month before the summer solstice and once a month afterward. Generally, that puts it in the latter part of May and the middle of July.

At the end of the day, the falling of the sun into the sea is best viewed from Hawai'i's western beaches, or, in the winter, from southern beaches. Views are also good from high-rise apartments, but a sunset in Hawai'i is best seen from near the sea.

A favorite challenge is to view the Green Flash. Some folks contend this phenomenon doesn't exist. Others insist they've seen several. And scientists have a range of explanations for it, ranging from a reaction that exists purely in the human optical system, to the prismatic bending of the sun's light by the earth's atmosphere. In any case, in order to be in a position to see it, you need the sun to set on a cloud-free horizon, so you can view the edge of Old Sol's upper limb as it disappears.

Hawai'i and the rest of the world got a gift of fine sunsets from the eruption of the Philippine volcano, Pinatubo, which filled our planet's atmosphere with its dust. The dust created spectacular optical effects at the end of the day, with deep red-orange sunset shows as the sun's light reflected off the dust. There's less of the dust with each passing year, but in Hawai'i we have our own volcanoes, and on those odd occasions when the winds are light and the volcanic haze covers the State, we can have sunsets the rest of the world can't match.

Kalalau Beach on Kaua'i is viewed at sunset, looking southwest along the Na Pali Coast.

'Alau Island stands in an orange sea at sunrise off Hana.

The sun sets on the tidepools and shallow shoreline waters of Ka'upulehu on Hawai'i.